Think about it...
Time

Harry Cory Wright

W
FRANKLIN WATTS
LONDON • SYDNEY

How might this street have changed in the last few hundred years?

How might this place
change over the year?

What would it be like
to sit quietly in this
room for a while?

When might you want to
have balloons?

Why do we celebrate birthdays?

What would it be like to see this at the beginning of the day?

How many of these items can you memorise in two minutes?

Why is this such fun?

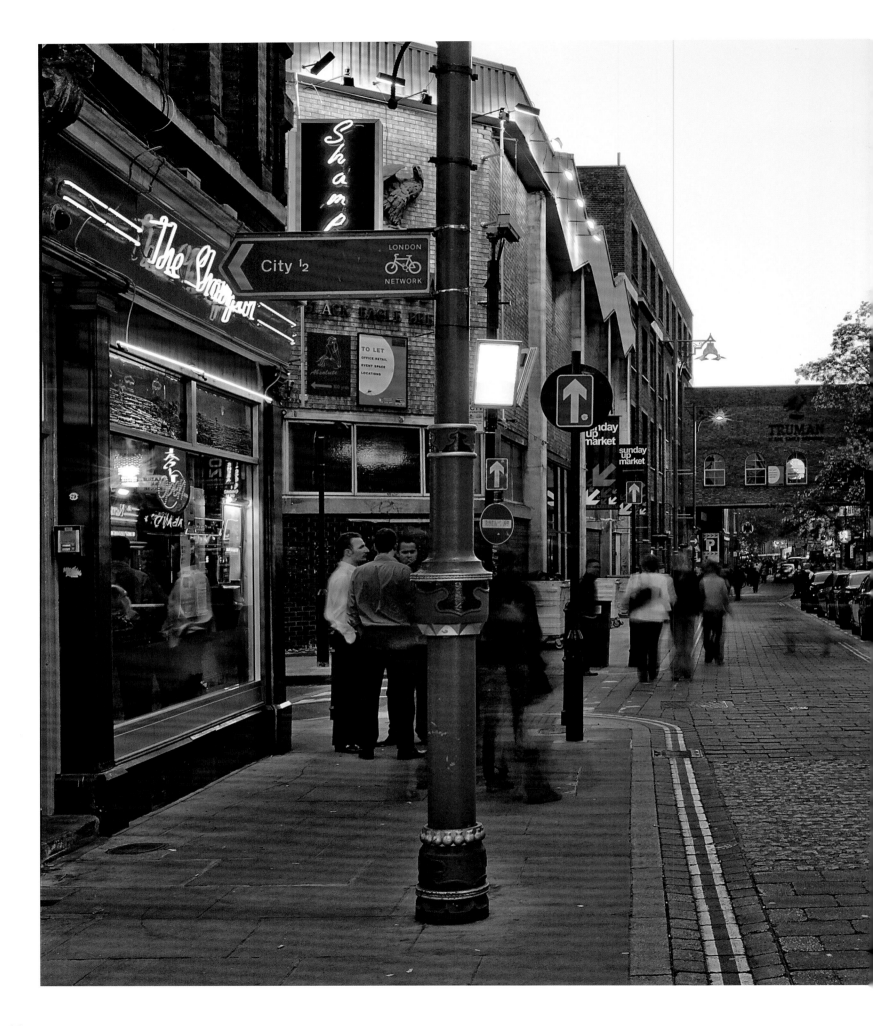

How might
this place have
changed over the
last 100 years?

What makes these people look different
from how we all look today?

What might people have carried in
this old fashioned luggage?

How long do you think it
would take to make this
sculpture?

What would take you a
long time to make?

How have toys changed since this one was made?

What do you think this man looked like as a boy?

What do you think people might think about this building
in 100 years' time?

What differences can you think of between the old church and this new building?

How were they built?

Would you like to spend the day here? Why?

Time

Time passes by and often we think little about it, but it's what gives us variety and change. Things grow with time and flourish. A gentle awareness of time is a good thing and here we explore all manner of possibilities, both simple and more intricate. Use the starting questions to begin to open the children's minds to how they might perceive and describe such a huge theme as 'Time'.

A framework for exploration

'What's going on in this picture?' is a question that is asked by children and adults alike whenever presented with a photograph. Usually the answer is in the caption. But what if we ask questions rather than provide answers? What if there is no right answer? The photographs in this book are intended to be starting points for children to explore ideas. Remember, there are no rules here, let alone any right answers – children can take a simple idea and run with it as far as they wish.

The teacher or parent should use his or her judgement to decide the appropriate depth of discussion according to the abilities of the child. Some children may describe only what they see in the picture in clear sentences. Other children should be able to extend the themes and offer in depth explanations and opinions. Ideas for expanding each theme are listed below in 'Talk about', but you may also ask some general questions on the theme of time such as: in what ways do we mark the passing of time?

How might this street have changed in the last few hundred years? (pages 2–3)
This street is in Norwich and is famous for being much like it was a long time ago.
Talk about: • how streets have changed • if the street would have been busier in the past • what it would be like on market day today and 200 years ago • the sorts of things people would buy in a street like this.

How might this place change over the year? (pages 4–5)
This is a garden where we used to live.
Talk about: • what the garden would be like the next day as it warmed up • how it would change if it got colder • what it would be like to play in the garden • how the garden may look in other seasons • which is their favourite season and why.

What would it be like to sit quietly in this room for a while? (pages 6–7)
This is the front room of some friends of mine. It's a very simple room and they love it. It is very much like it was about 50 years ago... maybe more. It's very quiet and you can hear the noises outside in the farmyard.
Talk about: • how and why rooms change over time • what makes this room look old-fashioned • what things they would like to stay the same • what things they would like to add to the room and why.

When might you want to have balloons? (page 8)
Balloons evoke celebrations and fun for some reason. Why is this?
Talk about: • why we use balloons on special occasions • why we want to celebrate things • what other items remind us of special times • if any of the children dislike balloons and why.

Why do we celebrate birthdays? (pages 8–9)
This is my daughter Katherine's birthday.
Talk about: • why we celebrate birthdays • how birthday celebrations change as you get older and why that is • the bits that remain the same • favourite festivals and celebrations through the year.

What would it be like to see this at the beginning of the day? (pages 10–11)

This is a view of a sunrise on the South Downs in England. It was very early in the morning and the birds were singing loudly. It always feels very much like a beginning when I photograph the sunrise.

Talk about: • how seeing a sunrise might affect you through the day • how the sky changes through the day and what causes this • why clear skies are nicer to see than cloudy ones.

How many of these items can you memorise in two minutes? (pages 12–13)

This is a very messy drawer in our house. I haven't really rearranged anything. I have just taken a few of the big things out. Can you make up stories about some of these things?

Talk about: • how quickly time seems to pass when you are given a task to do like this • where the things all come from • how some of the things were made • why people sometimes hold onto things they don't use for a long time.

Why is this such fun? (pages 14–15)

These are some friends of mine playing on a beach.

Talk about: • why this looks like fun • if it had been you doing this, would you remember it that evening? • would you remember it in a few years' time? • fun times they have had in the past that they will always remember.

How might this place have changed over the last 100 years? (pages 16–17)

This is Brick Lane in London on a warm evening. It's a very multicultural place. Over the years different immigrant populations have settled in the area.

Talk about: • why people move to new places • why some people like to live with people from the same background • how might such an area change day to day and over the year • how different it would have looked 200 years ago and how it might look in another 200 years.

What makes these people look different from how we all look today? (page 18)

Why does each generation look different? This picture was taken in 1913, just before the First World War.

Talk about: • what makes them look different from a cricket team today and from young men today • why and how fashions change over time • what might have become of these men.

What might people have carried in this old fashioned luggage? (page 19)

These old suitcases are exhibits on a museum railway platform but once upon a time they were used properly.

Talk about: • what they might have carried and what kind of places they might have been taken to • how new cases differ from these old ones.

How long do you think it would take to make this sculpture? What would take you a long time to make? (pages 20–21)

This is a friend of mine working in his studio on a sculpture of a horse's head. He spends all his time making these and loves it with a passion.

Talk about: • things you make and how much time it can take up • things that are worth spending a lot of time doing • how 'talent' at something actually requires many hours of dedication.

How have toys changed since this one was made? (page 22)

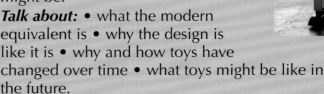

This robot toy from the 1950s/60s can be wound up to make it move. Modern copies of these old toys are popular – you could discuss why this might be.

Talk about: • what the modern equivalent is • why the design is like it is • why and how toys have changed over time • what toys might be like in the future.

What do you think this man looked like as a boy? (page 23)
This is a picture of myself taken a few years ago. Feel free to ask the children anything about me. Ask, perhaps, why I decided to make this book.
Talk about: • what this man might have looked like when he was younger • what he will look like later in life • how we all change as time goes by • how we are affected by what's around us.

What do you think people might think about this building in 100 years' time? (pages 24–25)
This building, the iconic Swiss Re building, fondly known as the Gherkin, is in the City of London.
Talk about: • what you think the building would be like inside • how it would differ from a building built 50 years ago, or even 100 years ago • if you think everyone likes it and why • why some people might not like it.

What differences can you think of between the old church and this new building? How were they built? (pages 26–27)
This 15th century church and the modern shopping centre it's viewed from are in Norwich. Many people use both buildings but how do you think the space differs in each?
Talk about: • how building materials have changed • how we use buildings differently today compared to 500 years ago.

Would you like to spend the day here? (pages 28–29)
This is a beach in Cornwall on a fine warm day. Some of the people are on holiday.
Talk about: what you would do here • games to play • how long you would spend here • whether you would return or find another beach • if life would be better if you only spent it on a beach.

First published in 2009
by Franklin Watts

Copyright © Harry Cory Wright 2009

Franklin Watts
338 Euston Road
London NW1 3BH

Franklin Watts Australia
Level 17/207 Kent Street
Sydney, NSW 2000

Series editor: Sarah Peutrill
Art director: Jonathan Hair
Consultant: Sue Graves

Dewey number: 529

ISBN 978 0 7496 8851 6

Printed in China

Franklin Watts is a division of Hachette Children's Books, an Hachette UK company.

www.hachette.co.uk